Eye Spy Colors

Debbie MacKinnon
Photographs by Anthea Sieveking

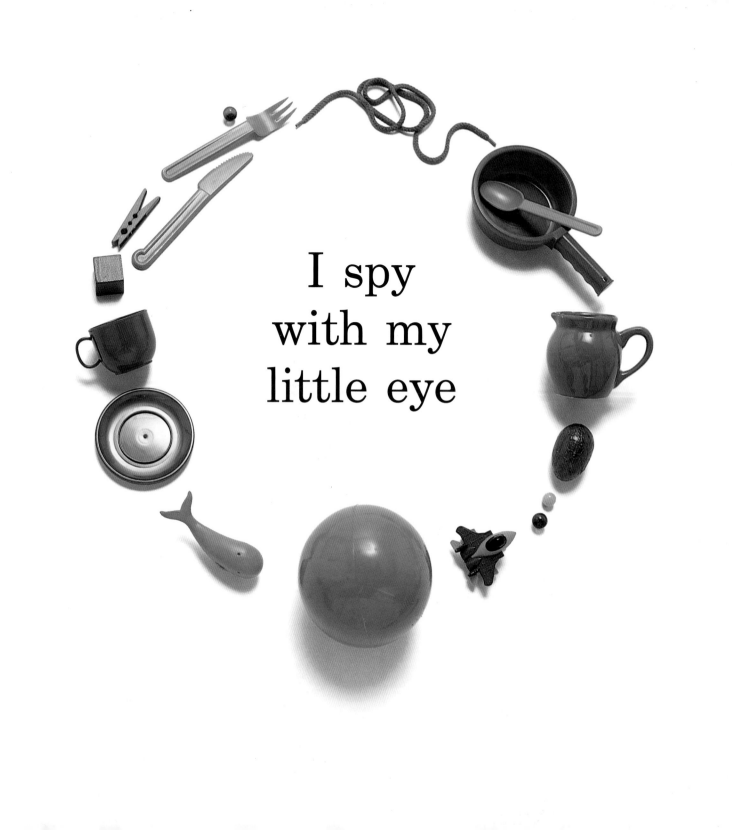

I spy
with my
little eye

something blue
and bouncy . . .

a blue
ball

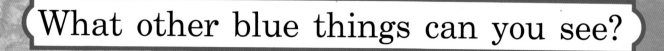

What other blue things can you see?

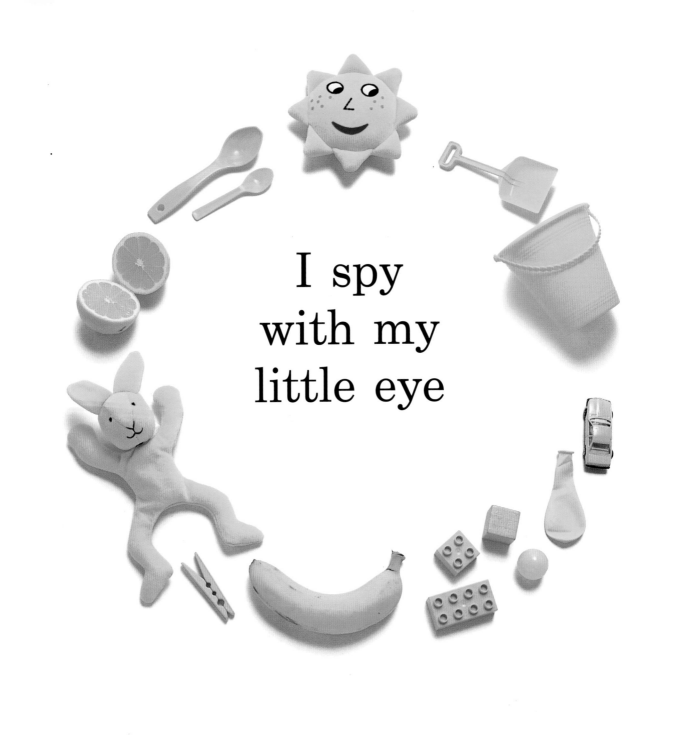

I spy
with my
little eye

something yellow
and sandy . . .

a yellow
bucket

What other yellow things can you see?

I spy
with my
little eye

something red
and crunchy . . .

red
apples

What other red things can you see?

I spy
with my
little eye

something green
and shiny . . .

a green
watering can

What other green things can you see?

I spy
with my
little eye

something orange
and fluffy . . .

an orange
towel